Bethlehem's Star

Written by

Paul F. Taylor

Just Six Days Publishing

Published by J6D Publications
PO Box 139
Naples, ID 83847
USA

ISBN (printed): 978-1-7337363-8-1

Printed by Amazon KDP.

Contents

01. A Wandering Star

A Wandering Star

Did you know the word planet was in the Bible?

"I was born under a wandering star"[1] sang Lee Marvin. The title does not necessarily imply occult connections, but refers to the medieval cosmological observation, whereby a date of birth would be recorded according to which constellation of the Mazzaroth (Zodiac) was rising at that part of the year. Each of the Mazzaroth constellations takes about 30 days to rise, and, by circuitous routes, gives us the length of our calendar months, which are a little longer than the lunar month of 28 days. Marvin's character, Ben Rumson, declares that he is born under a wandering star, to emphasize his nomadic nature. Of course, some stars do indeed wander, while others remain fixed. The wandering stars are few in number, and, in medieval cosmology, numbered seven in all – Luna (Moon), Mercury, Venus, Sol (Sun), Mars, Jupiter, and Saturn. The Greek names for these are Selene, Hermes, Aphrodite, Helios (or Apollo), Ares, Zeus, and Kronos. The Greek word for wandering star is Planetus (πλανήτης) - from which we get our word planet. And this word appears just

---

[1]   Lerner, A.J. and Loewe, F. (1951), *PaintYour Wagon, musical play, made into a movie in 1969, starring Lee Marvin, Clint Eastwood, and Jean Seberg.*

once in the New Testament.

In his epistle, Jude describes perverted people, who have infiltrated the church.

> These [people] are hidden reefs at your love feasts,
> as they feast with you without fear, shepherds
> feeding themselves; waterless clouds, swept along
> by winds; fruitless trees in late autumn, twice dead,
> uprooted; wild waves of the sea, casting up the
> foam of their own shame; wandering stars
> (πλανῆται, *planetai*), for whom the gloom of utter
> darkness has been reserved forever. (Jude 1:12-13,
> emphasis, and Greek word, added)

This would appear to suggest that planets are not good. In

fact, *planetus* is a morally neutral word. It is the restlessness of these pseudo-Christian infiltrators, which is being criticized; just as there is nothing inherently wrong with "wild waves", though the restlessness of doctrine is being criticized.

But I do not need to delve further into the teaching of Jude, as it is simply the existence of biblical knowledge about planets or wandering stars which I am seeking to establish.

I have heard a semi-blasphemous joke that Jesus was also born under a wandering star. However, the star of the Gospel depends for its existence and meaning on the Messiah, not the other way around. It is odd that Matthew's description of the star does not describe it as a planet, given that Jude knew the word. Perhaps the fact that Bethelehem's Star is not referred to as *planetus* tells us something important about the nature of this object – and we will say more on this later.

The Christmas Star

The Christmas Star is an essential part of our traditional Christmas.

Like many towns in the UK, Bridgend in Wales, where I lived for 15 years, held a competition among city center stores, to see which had the best Christmas decorations. The

competition was judged by the Mayor of Bridgend Town. One year, the Mayor was a Muslim. You are probably expecting me to say that the competition was a disaster that year. Quite the opposite. Mayor Hawas bemoaned the fact that so many supposedly "Christian" storekeepers had ignored traditional symbols of Christianity, and awarded the prize to the only store that had a traditional manger scene in its window display!

My mother always made her own manger scene. She used an old shoe box, and glued some straw into it, to represent the floor of a stable. The shoe box was covered with wrinkled parcel paper to represent stone. "The stable was in a cave", she asserted. The figures of Mary, Joseph, a few shepherds, animals, and three wise men were added, with the baby Jesus being placed in a food trough. Finally, a large star was fixed above the sideways-turned box.

My mother's annual creation was an act of devotion, so it might seem churlish to point out that some of those elements were unbiblical. So I will make the following observation before I close this introductory passage. When I write about the six days of the creation week, I lay down the law firmly on the Scriptural position. But when I get to Genesis 6 and talk about the nephilim, I get a little less dogmatic, as there are godly, biblically minded people who take differing views on the nature of the nephilim. The same applies to the nature of the Star, and the other elements of the traditional Christmas scene. I will relate to you, in these pages, what I think the Bible is saying about these matters, but these are secondary doctrinal issues, and I will not label you as a heretic for believing something different about what the Star was. I hope you will not label me as a heretic either.

02. What's Wrong with the Traditional Christmas Scene?

What's Wrong with the Traditional Christmas Scene?

As I am about to criticize the traditional Christmas scene, I had better explain the nature of my criticism. It is not a criticism of doubt.

I am not doubting that there was a star. The Bible clearly states that there was. I am not doubting that, after His birth, Mary laid Jesus in a manger. That is what Scripture says. There were shepherds, who came from the fields, where they lived, because we read that in God's word. And wise men came from the East bringing their gifts of gold, frankincense, and myrrh. However, these happenings were not concurrent. But does it matter that the Bible speaks the truth? Yes, it does. These events were historical and truthful, and all the Bible, Old and New Testaments, declare them.

There are some Christian leaders who are seeking to play down the truthfulness of these historical accounts. For example, popular mega-church pastor Andy Stanley said "Christianity doesn't hinge on the truth of the stories of the birth of Jesus. It really hinges on the resurrection of Jesus."[1]

---

[1]   Stanley, A. (2016), *Who Needs Christmas?*, quoted in *Mappes, 2019, < https://www.garbc.org/commentary/stanleys-*

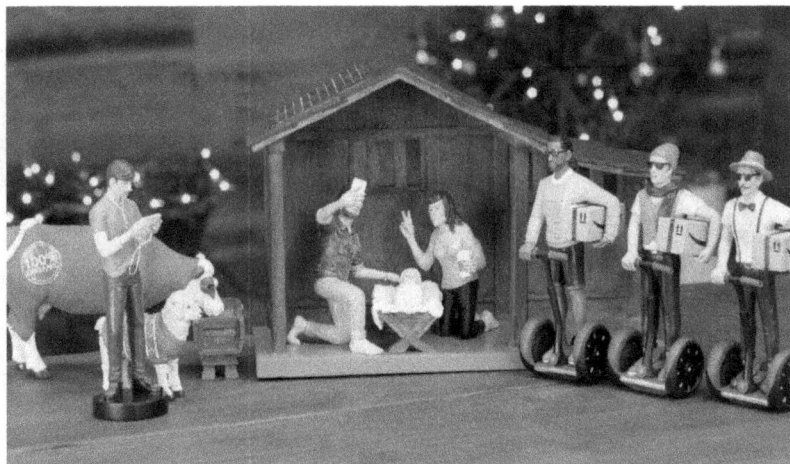

Although Stanley has since rowed back somewhat, and affirmed the traditional understanding of the virgin birth, his eisegesis is dangerous, and is part of his downgrading of the necessity of reading the Bible. In response, James R White said "It is not just about the resurrection of any individual. It is about the resurrection of the Incarnate Son of God"[2] Given that the first prophecy of the virgin birth of the Savior occurs immediately after the first sin (Genesis 3:15), we can see that the issue of the resurrection, in Genesis 3, and elsewhere, is

---

irresistible-is-a-dangerous-disappointment/ >, accessed 7/29/2021.

[2]   White, J.R. (2016), *The Dividing Line,* < *https://www.aomin.org/aoblog/general-apologetics/andy-stanley-separates-incarnation-redemption-paul-falsely-accused-tim-staples-reviewed/ >, accessed 7/29/2021.*

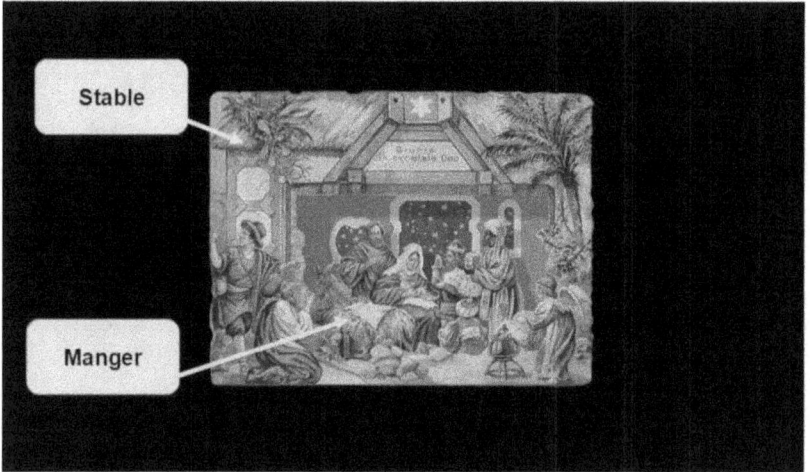

intimately interwoven with the issue of the incarnation.

So I am not casting doubt on the authenticity of any part of the Christmas story. I am simply showing that the events did not happen in quite the way that the traditional accounts state,

and, in my exegesis, I will start from Scripture, and stick with Scripture all the way through.

Picture the traditional Christmas scene, as found in many decorations. The scenes show a stable. Jesus was born in a stable, wasn't he? He was laid in a manger, because there was no room in the inn. Many elementary school plays picture the innkeeper apologizing for having no room. So he leads Joseph and Mary to his stable, which is either behind his inn, or perhaps in a nearby cave. The stable is full of straw and animals – the ox and ass keep watch.

> Why lies He in such mean estate
> Where ox and ass are feeding?
> Good Christian, fear, for sinners here
> The silent Word is pleading.[3]

Also present in the stable are a few shepherds, bringing a sheep. There will also be three Wise Men, often depicted as three kings, with their gifts of gold, frankincense, and myrrh. There will be a star over the stable; in fact, we should refer to this as The Star.

What can I give Him,

_____
[3]   Lyrics from the Carol *What Child Is This?*, by William C. Dix, *and usually sung to the tune Greensleeves.*

Poor as I am?
If I were a shepherd
I would bring a lamb,
If I were a wise man
I would do my part,
Yet what I can I give Him,

Give my heart.[4]

I am very fond of the Christmas Carols that I have quoted here and elsewhere. But that does not alter the fact that there are inaccuracies. The scene is not entirely biblical. Jesus, as a newborn, was indeed laid in a manger, but the Bible account does not mention a stable. Why was there no room in the inn? The reason is that it was not an inn. Joseph had family in Bethlehem, so it is likely that they went to stay with Joseph's family.

> And Joseph also went up from Galilee, from the town of Nazareth, to Judea, to the city of David, which is called Bethlehem, because he was of the house and lineage of David, to be registered with Mary, his betrothed, who was with child. (Luke 2:4-5)

Most houses of the time in the locality would have two

---

[4]   Lyrics from *In the Bleak Midwinter, by Christina Rosetti.*

floors. The guest quarters would be upstairs. The Greek words for these guest quarters is κατάλυμα (kataluma).

> And she gave birth to her firstborn son and wrapped him in swaddling cloths and laid him in a manger, because there was no place for them in the inn (kataluma). (Luke 2:7)

This word refers to the guest chamber, but has traditionally been translated as inn. This guest chamber is often an upper room. The word appears elsewhere in the Gospels. These were Jesus' instructions to His disciples on preparing for the Last Supper.

> Tell the master of the house, 'The Teacher says to you, Where is the guest room (kataluma), where I may eat the Passover with my disciples?' And he will show you a large upper room furnished; prepare it there. (Luke 22:11-12)

Downstairs, on ground level, would also be a place to live, but on colder evenings the household's animals would be brought in to feed, and provide some warmth for humans and animals alike. Thus it would be normal and natural, if the kataluma was crowded, for Joseph and Mary to go downstairs, where the animals would be feeding.

The Wise Men should not be there in the scene. The

shepherds arrived on the night of Jesus' birth, but, as I will show you, the Wise Men came about two years later. Joseph and Mary were still living in Bethlehem, but were no longer in the "stable", having got a house of their own. The Star was therefore in place for the visit of the Wise Men, not for the visit of the shepherds.

Since it is the Wise Men who are being wrongly associated with the day of Jesus' birth, we need to examine the biblical passage which refers to their coming.

03. Who Were the Wise Men?

(1) Now after Jesus was born in Bethlehem of Judea in the days of Herod the king, behold, wise men from the east came to Jerusalem,

(2) saying, "Where is he who has been born king of the Jews? For we saw his star when it rose and have come to worship him."

(3) When Herod the king heard this, he was troubled, and all Jerusalem with him;

(4) and assembling all the chief priests and scribes of the people, he inquired of them where the Christ was to be born.

(5) They told him, "In Bethlehem of Judea, for so it is written by the prophet:

(6) "'And you, O Bethlehem, in the land of Judah, are by no means least among the rulers of Judah; for from you shall come a ruler who will shepherd my people Israel.'"

(7) Then Herod summoned the wise men secretly and ascertained from them what time the star had appeared.

(8) And he sent them to Bethlehem, saying, "Go and search diligently for the child, and when you have found him, bring me word, that I too may come and worship him."

(9) After listening to the king, they went on their way. And behold, the star that they had seen when it rose went before them until it came to rest over the place where the child was.

(10) When they saw the star, they rejoiced exceedingly with great joy.

(11) And going into the house, they saw the child with Mary his mother, and they fell down and worshiped him. Then, opening their treasures, they offered him gifts, gold and frankincense and myrrh.

(12) And being warned in a dream not to return to Herod, they departed to their own country by another way.

It would seem that there are two questions that we need to address, in order fully to understand what is going on. These are:

1.What was the star?

2.Who were the wise men?

I will tackle these questions in reverse order.

The Greek word, which is translated as Wise Men, is μάγος (*magos*). We should note that they did not make their way directly to where Jesus' family lived, but rather went to Jerusalem. This gives us a clue to their identity. For now, I want you to notice that the Bible does not say how many Wise Men there were. The word is plural, so there must have been at least two. However, it is very unlikely that there were just two. Indeed, it is very unlikely that there were just three. Some traditions suggest that there were twelve, but even this number is, I suggest, too small. Why? Notice that in Matthew 2:3, Herod was troubled. Indeed, all of Jerusalem was troubled> How would just three Wise Men trouble this ruthless, violent king so much – a king that was fully prepared to murder his own son, in order to retain power. For this reason, I suggest that the whole retinue of Wise Men was very large, and they were possibly armed. Think in terms of at least a hundred Wise Men. Also, you should note that Wise Men were not kings.

They were akin to modern scientists, though the word, often rendered *magi* (μαγοι) is the root word for magician. In an age of early scientists, they were probably into alchemy, and certainly into astrology, even if we want to think it was more akin to modern astronomy. In this time period, such people would not have recognized a difference between astrology and astronomy. They clearly studied stars, and came from the East. From where could they have come, if they were from the East? People from the East world probably have been from Babylon.

Herod's reaction is also informative for us. Notice that

Herod wanted to know the exact time of the appearance of the star. Why? He clearly knew that this would give him the date of birth of this baby king. In Matthew 2:7, we read that he got this information. He then wanted to know from the Wise Men the exact location of where Jesus was born. Given what Herod did later, we can consider that it was a good thing that the Magi did not know that location, and this must be part of God's Sovereign provision in this entire episode. What the Magi did not know was partially filled in by Herod's counsellors, who showed that the Messiah had to born in the nearby city of Bethlehem. As we know, the Magi did not return to Herod, so this wicked king subsequently had all baby boys in Bethlehem two years and under killed. This suggests that the Magi had

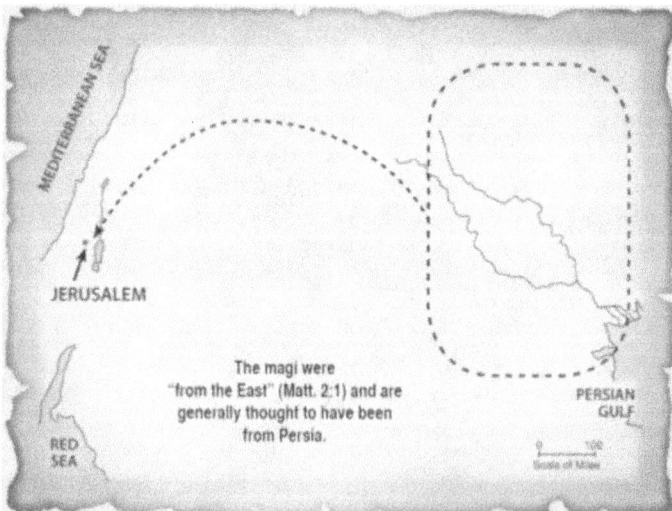

The magi were "from the East" (Matt. 2:1) and are generally thought to have been from Persia.

told Herod that the star had appeared two years previously, and therefore Jesus was no longer a babe in arms; He was a two-year-old toddler. In our next section, we will also need to note that the Magi did not follow a star to Jerusalem. They had simply seen the star, when it appeared at Jesus' birth, and we can assume that it was no longer visible. More on this in chapter 4. For now, we can assume that the Magi made their way to Jerusalem, not knowing where Jesus had been born, because it was logical to go to Israel's capital.

Are there any Wise Men mentioned previously in the Bible? The answer is yes! There were Wise Men in Babylon in Daniel's time. It is too much of a coincidence to see these as a different group, as I will now show. And, of course, Daniel saved the lives of the Wise Men of his day. These Wise Men visiting Jesus must have been of the same school as those familiar to Daniel.

The wise men are mentioned in Daniel 2. Of course, we are dealing with a different language, as most of Daniel was written in Hebrew, with some sections in Aramaic. We should note that Daniel and his three companions were already counted among the wise men. The Hebrew word is *chakkîym* (חַכִּים), which is derived from the term for Chaldeans, so the chapter refers both to Chaldeans and Wise Men as synonymous. However, so that we can make a better comparison, it will be instructive to look at the Septuagint, which is given the abbreviation LXX. The LXX is a Greek translation of the Old Testament, begun in the 3ʳᵈ Century BC. The Greek word used for Wise Men in Daniel 2 is σοφοὺς (*sophous*), so this appears to ruin our use of Daniel 2. But we find that members of the Wise Men included such skills as magicians and enchanters (Daniel 2:10), referred to in the KJV as magicians and astrologers. The single word used in the LXX for magicians and astrologers is *magos* (μάγος)! So the skills possessed by these Wise Men are exactly those summed up by the word, which is used in Matthew's Gospel for these Wise Men. It is safe, therefore, to state that Daniel's Wise Men are of the same school that later voyaged to Jerusalem, because they saw a special star.

The story of Daniel 2, briefly, is this. Nebuchadnezzar, the King of Babylon, had a very bad dream. He called some of his Wise Men and commanded them to interpret his dream, but refused to tell them what the dream was – they had to tell him dream and interpretation. As a quick bunny trail, we can note that Daniel, on hearing about the problem, took two important courses of action, that we should emulate today. First, he sought the counsel of his three Godly companions, Hananiah, Mishael, and Azariah, and, second, they all prayed. God revealed both dream and interpretation to Daniel, who told Nebuchadnezzar. The dream was of the statue and the four empires, but I am not going down that bunny trail at the moment. The upshot of Daniel's revelation to Nebuchadnezzar – for which he rightly gave all the glory to God – was that Daniel was made into a sort of Assistant King, and the Wise Men were spared. Do you think this event had an effect on the Wise Men? I would suggest the effect was great and profound. It is very likely that many Wise Men became worshipers of the true God. Daniel was not only made ruler over Babylon, under the King, but was also made chief prefect of the Wise Men. He would have been responsible for training these Wise Men. So when, many years later, Daniel was given his own visions, it is likely that these were also shared with his Wise Men.

> Know therefore and understand, that from the going forth of the commandment to restore and to build Jerusalem unto the Messiah the Prince shall be seven weeks, and threescore and two weeks: the street shall be built again, and the wall, even in troublous times. And after threescore and two weeks shall Messiah be cut off, but not for himself:

and the people of the prince that shall come shall destroy the city and the sanctuary; and the end thereof shall be with a flood, and unto the end of the war desolations are determined. (Daniel 9:25-26 KJV)

The prophecy of Daniel 9 refers to the Anointed One, as some versions translate it. The Hebrew word is *mâshîyach* (מָשִׁיחַ), and the Greek word in the LXX is χριστοῦ (*Christ*). The passage refers to 7 weeks, then 62 weeks. These "weeks" can be seen as periods of seven years, not days, so the time period from this event to the death of the Messiah ("Messiah shall be cut off") can be calculated. The exact length of Hebrew years can be discussed elsewhere, and there are various theories. The only point I would make here is that this passage suggests approximately when the death of the Messiah would be, **and the Wise Men would have known this information!**

Of course, this Scripture does not reveal how old the Messiah would be when he died. The Wise Men would not have known exactly when Messiah would be born, so they would probably have started looking out for signs of Messiah's birth approximately 70 years before the date He was due to die. This would have been from about the year that we now call 40BC.

But what sign would they have been looking for?

We should look back at two other prophecies that Daniel could have made known to the Wise Men. First, let us look at the prophecies Jacob spoke over his children – in particular, Jacob's oracle over Judah, who would eventually be the lead tribe of Israel, and the tribe from which Jesus came.

> The scepter shall not depart from Judah, nor the
> ruler's staff from between his feet, until tribute
> comes to him; and to him shall be the obedience of
> the peoples. (Genesis 49:10)

A scepter was, and still is, a symbol of kingship – far more so than a crown. So Jacob's prophecy makes clear that the Messiah was to come from the tribe of Judah.

Now, couple this oracle with another one. In Numbers 22 – 25, we meet a strange semi-pagan prophet named Balaam. Balaam was hired by the Balak, son of Zippor, to curse the Israelites. But every time Balaam tried to curse Israel, he ended up blessing them instead. Balaam was said to come from Pethor, near the River, which refers to the Euphrates. If Balaam were not from Babylon, he was certainly from that region, and it is likely that his words were known by the Wise Men, both from Daniel and from traditions passed down among earlier Wise Men.

Balaam's fourth and final oracle is particularly noteworthy.

> I see him, but not now; I behold him, but not near: a star shall come out of Jacob, and a scepter shall rise out of Israel; it shall crush the forehead of Moab and break down all the sons of Sheth. (Numbers 24:17)

Once again, we have mention of the kingly scepter. But we also hear that "a star shall come out of Jacob". This is a prophecy that the Wise Men would have picked up on, probably delivered by one of their own spiritual ancestors. And, remember, the Wise Men were astrologers/astronomers. Therefore, I believe that when the Wise Men went on high alert, looking for the sign of Messiah's coming, it was a star that they were looking for. So, at the very moment of Jesus' birth, they did indeed spot an unusual star, and knew that the Messiah had been born. So they made their preparations to travel to Jerusalem, in the land of Judah, to find the Messiah and worship Him.

Before we leave the subject of the Wise Men, in order to turn our attention to the Star, it would be instructive to consider what the Wise Men did not know. They did not know the prophecy of Micah, as it is unlikely that Daniel knew it either.

But you, O Bethlehem Ephrathah, who are too little to be among the clans of Judah, from you shall come forth for me one who is to be ruler in Israel, whose coming forth is from of old, from ancient days. (Micah 5:2)

If they had known this prophecy, they would have gone straight to Bethlehem, rather than Jerusalem. However, it was God's plan for this huge "army" of Wise Men to go to Jerusalem, be seen by the people, and meet Herod. The fact that they did not go straight to Bethlehem tells us two things. They did not know Micah's prophecy, and had to be told by Herod's people. But also it tells us that the Star was not guiding them from Babylon to Jerusalem. I believe that the star appeared only briefly in Babylon, and they did not see it again, until the surprising incident, when the star led the, from Jerusalem to Bethlehem.

> After listening to the king, they went on their way. And behold, the star that they had seen **when it rose** went before them until it came to rest over the place where the child was. (Matthew 2:9, emphasis added)

It is now time to study the Star itself, and work out what we think it could have been.

04. What Was the Star?

Many people have wondered what exactly Bethlehem's Star was. What are stars anyway? In the Voyage of the Dawn Treader, the characters meet a "retired" star, called Ramandu. The idea of a star being a person is a problem to the most materialistic of the characters.

> "In our world," said Eustace, "a star is a huge ball of flaming gas."

> [Ramandu replied] "Even in your world, my son, that is not what a star is, but only what it is made of."[1]

The author of the above – C.S. Lewis – was a great fan of Mediæval Cosmology, as he described in his last (non-fictional) book, The Discarded Image. In that work, Lewis showed that the mediæval scholar had a wealth of understanding of what stars were. He actually dismissed the charge that we can have no use for medieval cosmology, because it has been superseded scientifically.

> I have made no serious effort to hide the fact that the old Model delights me as I believe it delighted

[1]   Lewis, C.S. (1952), The Voyage of the Dawn Treader.

our ancestors. Few constructions of the imagination seem to me to have combined splendour, sobriety, and coherence in the same degree. It is possible that some readers have long been itching to remind me that it had a serious defect; it was not true. I agree. It was not true. But I would like to end by saying that this charge can no longer have exactly the same sort of weight for us

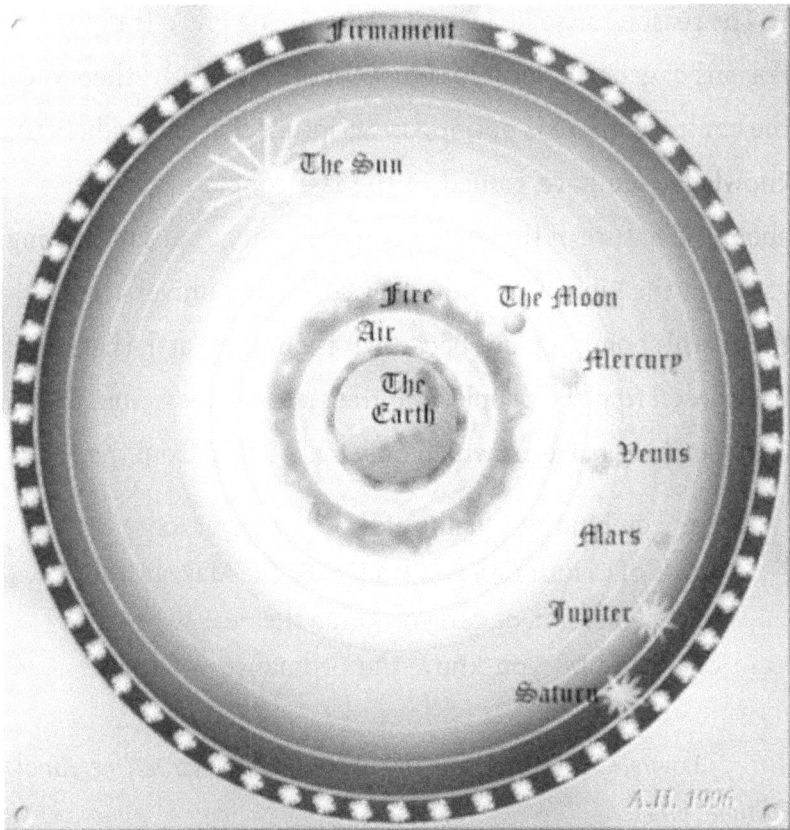

that it would have had in the nineteenth century.[2]

It is clear that, in the Bible, a star have more meaning than simply being "a huge ball of flaming gas". It is always a shock to see how little space is left in Genesis 1 to the creation of the stars.

He also made the stars... (Genesis 1:16 NLT)

The reason for so little information being given is not for reasons of geocentricity or some sort of "flat earth" theory. On the contrary, there is nothing in Scripture that contradicts the knowledge we have gained in the last couple of centuries about the nature of the stars – Eustace's "huge balls of flaming gas". But the Bible is unashamedly seeing the universe from the Earth's point of view, because it is only on Earth that God has chosen to place people, and the stars are seen from the Earth, making patterns which only make sense from the Earth.

"Can you bind the chains of the Pleiades or loose the cords of Orion? Can you lead forth the Mazzaroth in their season, or can you guide the Bear with its children? Do you know the ordinances of the

[2]   Lewis, C.S. (2013), *The Discarded Image*, (HarperOne: Kindle Edition), p.111.

heavens? Can you establish their rule on the earth?"
(Job 38:31-33)

The heavens declare the glory of God, and the sky
above proclaims his handiwork. (Psalms 19:1)

"And there will be signs in sun and moon and stars,
and on the earth distress of nations in perplexity
because of the roaring of the sea and the waves,
people fainting with fear and with foreboding of
what is coming on the world. For the powers of the
heavens will be shaken." (Luke 21:25-26)

Nothing in Scripture is in opposition to what we have
learned about the nature and movement of stars. Of course,
much in Scripture is opposed to modern concepts of
cosmogony – that is, how the universe came to be. Though
there are few different theories of cosmogony developed by
biblical Christians, it is important to note that our starting
point must always be the words of Scripture. While there is
much in medieval cosmology that we will not accept as fact
today, we should note that their cosmology did not differ with
a biblical cosmogony. For the most part, medieval scholars
accepted the truth of the biblical account of creation. So, when
they ascribed meaning to the medieval planets, while they

may have inherited characteristics from Roman and Greek paganism, their descriptors are not opposed to Christianity any more than is Big Bang cosmogony. Medieval scholars were not proposing to worship these planets.

All this discussion brings us to the important question of the various theories about the Bethlehem Star. I suggest five possible candidates.

1.Jupiter or Venus

2.A Conjunction

3.A Supernova

4.A Comet

Venus is the brightest object in the sky, after the Sun and the Moon. Its brightness is due to two factors; firstly, at its nearest point in its orbit of the Sun, it is the closest planet to the Earth., and secondly, it is completely covered with opaque clouds, which are highly reflective of sunlight. The planets do not have light of their own. They shine on Earth, because of the reflection of the Sun's light.

In medieval thought, Venus (Aphrodite to the Greeks) is associated with love and femininity, as she was to the pagans. However, much poetry also associates her with beauty and with creation. Venus had, at one time, been considered as two stars – Venus and Aurora; the latter name meaning Dawn, and indicating a difference between morning and evening stars. When cultures realized that these were appearances of the same planet, some cultures noticed that there were three days between the disappearance of the Morning Star and the appearance of the Evening Star. This allusion is suggestive of Jesus' identification with the term *morning star* in the New Testament – notably in 2 Peter 1:19 and Revelation 22:16. Of course, the term morning star is also famously associated with Satan, from its appearance in Isaiah 14:12 (especially using the Latin form Lucifer). The fact that the same term can be used of

Jesus and the devil is indicative of Satan's works of deception.

Even Satan disguises himself as an angel of light. (2 Corinthians 11:14)

Michael Ward, in his excellent book *Planet Narnia*, emphasizes Lewis's use of the Venereal in creation. He quotes from *The Magicians Nephew.*

> The Lion opened his mouth, but no sound came from it; he was breathing out, a long, warm breath; it seemed to sway all the beasts as the wind sways a line of trees. Far overhead overhead from beyond the veil of blue sky which hid them the stars sang again: a pure, cold, difficult music. Then there came a swift flash of fire (but it burnt nobody) either from the sky or from the Lion itself, and every drop of blood tingled in the children's bodies, and the deepest, wildest voice they had ever heard was saying: 'Narnia, Narnia, Narnia, awake. Love.'[3]

There is a direct allusion to fertility in Genesis 1, when we read that Adam and Eve were to "Be fruitful and multiply and fill the earth and subdue it" (Genesis 1:28). Our falsely-placed modesty allows us to overlook this aspect of creation, but

[3]   Lewis, C.S. (), *The Magician's Nephew, HarperOne, p.108.*

Ward unashamedly comments thus:

> With respect to the creation of Narnia, the whole
> creating process should be seen as a Venereal
> accomplishment, but it will be useful to focus on
> specific images which Lewis commonly used in his
> depictions of Venus. Just as in his 1935 poem he
> had written of 'grass growing, and grain bursting, /
> Flower unfolding,' so, at the birth of Narnia, all
> these features receive a mention, directly or
> indirectly. 'Grain bursting' is alluded to in the
> hymn which the Cabby sings in the darkness, 'all
> about crops being "safely gathered in"': the hymn
> is Henry Alford's 'Come, Ye Thankful People, Come'
> and contains a prayer that worshippers will be
> 'wholesome grain and pure.' The 'grass growing' is
> referenced more explicitly than the grain: we are
> told that 'the valley grew green with grass. It ran
> up the sides of the little hills like a wave. In a few
> minutes it was creeping up the lower slopes of the
> distant mountains, making that young world every
> moment softer.[4]

Jupiter also shines light on the Earth by virtue of reflected

---

[4]   Ward, Michael. Planet Narnia (pp. 181-182). Oxford
University Press. Kindle Edition.

sunlight. It is also by far the largest of the planets, big enough to have more volume than all the other planets combined, including Saturn. Jupiter, sometimes referred to as Jove, had a nature which was both jovial and kingly to the medieval mind. Lewis refers to Jupiter therefore being confused with his maker, in *That Hideous Strength,* and his friend and fellow Inkling, Charles Williams, referred to Jupiter's Great Red Spot as being a wound, like the wounds of Christ. There even seems to be a sort-of allusion to this in the Bible. In Genesis 14:17-24, we meet an unusual character, called Melchizedek king of

Salem. One possible translation of the name Melchizedek is "King of Jupiter". Unlike Venus, Jupiter could appear at any time of night, so might be a better candidate for Bethlehem's Star. But the principle problem with accepting either of these as the star in Matthew 2 is that the movements and appearances of both have been known to the ancient world for a very, very long time. The Wise Men, as highly proficient astronomers / astrologers, would hardly have been surprised at the appearance of either planet, and would surely not have considered either to be a cause for undertaking a major journey.

Before I leave these planets behind, I want to give a bit of a personal testimony. Christmas was always a special time of year for me. In my early childhood, my family attended an ancient Anglican church in Ashton-under-Lyne, called St. Michael and All Angels. On the Sunday before Christmas, the Evensong service would be a "Festival of Nine Lessons and Carols". The "lessons" were readings from the Bible, which included the important Old Testament prophecies and the Gospel accounts. Each lesson was read by a different "dignity". For example, the penultimate lesson (Matthew 2) was always read by the Mayor of the town, while the last lesson (John 1)

was read by the Rector. The first lesson was Genesis 3:8-19, which includes the important *Protengelium* – first Gospel – of Genesis 3:15. This lesson was always read by the Head Choirboy. And in 1972, the Head Choirboy was me, so I made my way to the high double-decker pulpit, and, in a squeaky voice, read the "lesson" which would be so influential on my later life and work.

But in 1976, my parents decided to leave that church, for reasons which need not detain us here. Instead, we began to attend another Anglican church; this time in our home town of Stalybridge, called Holy Trinity. Anyone who knows anything about the Church of England will know that it is a three-legged stool! There are three kinds of parishes. Some are traditional, fairly liberal. Some are Anglo-Catholic, often seeming to be more Catholic than the Roman Catholics. But some are Gospel-preaching, Bible-believing churches. St. Michael's had been Type 1. Holy Trinity was definitely Type 3. So, despite having gone to church since my infancy, I now heard the Gospel for the first time. Very soon, it was the Sunday before Christmas 1976. The Vicar preached the Gospel. I do not remember much of the sermon, but I remembered and

I understood when he said that God had no grandchildren. I had to repent of my sin and trust in Jesus my Savior. That week, we also went to church on Christmas Eve, for a Midnight Communion service. This short service began at 11:00pm, and finished at Midnight, as Christmas Day began. Again, I do not remember the sermon, but I do know that I knew for sure that I was not a Christian, and that I needed to be one. It is difficult to explain how my 15-year-old mind worked. I was puzzled, yet excited at the same time. Just to jump ahead; I do not know exactly when I was saved, but I know that at the Good Friday and Easter Sunday services of 1977, I was definitely saved. So I was saved sometime between Christmas 1976 and Easter 1977.

But back to the Midnight Communion, 1976. As we left the church, to cross the parking lot, I looked up at the beautiful clear sky, and saw a bright star. Years later, I have worked out that it was the planet Jupiter. I have even been able to trace my view of the sky that night from that churchyard, using Stellarium software. Don't get me wrong. I never for one minute thought that the star that I saw – Jupiter – was Bethlehem's Star. But for my personal life, it was my personal Bethlehem's Star, that convinced me once and for all that the Gospel was true, and let to my inevitable salvation a couple of weeks later.

2A Conjunction

If the Star was not one of the bright planets, then perhaps it was a conjunction of two or three planets, making an even brighter astronomical object. This would also be a more unusual astronomical event and would perhaps pique the interest of the Wise Men.

In June 2015, there was a conjunction of both the planets mentioned above, making a very bright object indeed. This was interesting, because the planetary discs appeared to touch – an event which had not occurred since 3BC. That interesting triple conjunction of Jupiter, Venus, and the fixed star Regulus, was the subject of Frederick Larson's talk *The Star of Bethlehem*, in which he proposed that this conjunction, coupled with the

planetary movements through various constellations, must have been the event referred to in Matthew 2.

Let me say immediately that Larson's idea is feasible, and is certainly in line with Scripture. However, even when the planetary discs appear to touch, there is still a bit of a distance between them. In none of these conjunctions do the objects appear to "fuse" into one object. For this reason, I do not accept this model – though you are not heretical if you disagree with me! Larson worked through his model in a biblical manner.

3A Supernova

A nova is a "new" star. In practice, it is a star that has exploded. A supernova is such a big explosion that the star could change in brightness from being too faint to see to becoming as bright as Venus and then fading away again. A supernova would certainly catch the attention of the Wise Men.

Supernovae have also been detected by other ancient recorders. For example, Chinese and Korean records suggest that there was a supernovae event recorded on February 23rd in the year 4 BC. This would certainly be within the accepted timescale, as early errors in the Western calendar mean that

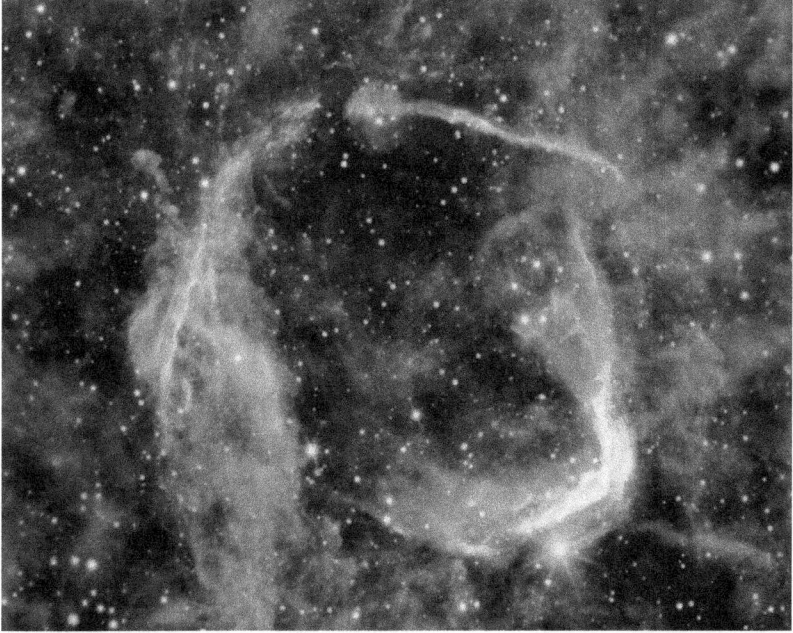

the birth of Jesus might not have been 1 AD, but could have been as early as 7 BC at the extreme, with 4 BC being the most favored date.

My reasons for rejecting the supernova theory really relate to the behavior of the Bethlehem Star. A supernova could not be an object that moved and allowed Wise Men to follow. A supernova is certainly a possible theory, but does not strike me as the best explanation, as I will explain later.

4A Comet
The idea of a comet as Bethlehem's Star is a more popular

idea. And the most popular comet candidate would be Halley's Comet.

The most recent appearance of Halley's Comet was 1986. It was not a spectacular appearance. For me, a much more memorable comet appearance was that of Hale-Bopp in 1997. But in 1986, I was a schoolteacher in Ashton-under-Lyne, near Manchester, England. One of my ministries at the time was

that I edited a small creationist newsletter called *Rainbow*. I wrote a couple of articles in the newsletter about the comet, and how it could be observed. As its period is 75 or 76 years, it will not return until 2061, when I do not expect to be around!

Halley's Comet was discovered by Edmond Halley, a contemporary of Isaac Newton, in 1682. Haley's calculations led him to predict that it would return in 1758. Unfortunately, Halley died in 1742, but his prediction turned out to be correct, when the comet did indeed just make 1758, by returning in December of that year.

With such accurate calculations, it is easy to work back to previous comet appearances and determine that some of those, also, were actually Halley's Comet. One famous appearance was in 1066, and nearly spared England its conquest by William of Normandy, as Norman forces were said to have interpreted the comet as a bad omen. Tradition suggests that the Duke of Normandy persuaded his followers that the comet was a bad omen for the Saxons, and the invasion of England proceeded as planned, with success. The comet is illustrated on the Bayeaux Tapestry.

Perhaps less well known is the appearance of Halley's Comet in 1301. It was probably seen by the artist Giotto di

Bondone. He painted a cycle of illustrations in the Scrovegni Chapel, at Padua, Italy. His Nativity section shows a stable, with a fiery comet as the Star.

Is it possible that Bethlehem's Star was a comet? It is unlikely. Halley's Comet would, actually, be the closest candidate, but its appearance was in 12 BC, which is just too early, even allowing for calendar errors.

5None of the Above

This leads us to the final theory, which needs a chapter of its own.

05. Not an Astronomical Object

Since we have mentioned medieval cosmology a few times, we should be clear that people in those centuries would almost certainly have considered Bethlehem's Star to be a supernatural object. Why should we not consider that as a valid explanation?

Consider, for example, these points.

> And being warned in a dream not to return to Herod, they departed to their own country by another way. Now when they had departed, behold, an angel of the Lord appeared to Joseph in a dream and said, "Rise, take the child and his mother, and flee to Egypt, and remain there until I tell you, for Herod is about to search for the child, to destroy him." (Matthew 2:12-13)

We have already discussed that the Father's revelation of His Son's right of kingship was supernatural. In Matthew 2:12-13, we have two very clearly supernatural events. The return journey of the Wise Men was supernaturally guided, by a warning which occurred in a dream. If there were, as I suggest, a hundred or so Wise Men, then did they all get the dream, or just one? We have no way of knowing. Either way, they did not find their way home by means of GPS. Immediately after the Wise Men had departed, Joseph got a dream, in which an angel told him to take his wife and child to Egypt. How long they stayed there, we do not know. What we do know is that their return to Nazareth was also by supernatural guidance, as the angel told Joseph that he would tell him when to return.

Given that so many events in this historic account were supernatural, I wonder why so many people spend time searching for naturalistic explanations for the Star.

The Greek word which is translated as star is *aster (αστηρ)*. That this word is the root for other words to do with stars seems clear. Words such as astronomy, astrology, and astronaut are all derived from aster. However, the ancient Greeks did not know that the stars were "huge balls of flaming gas". So the word aster does not exclusively refer to a star. It can refer to any glowing object that can be seen in the sky, or even in the atmosphere. For example, ball lightning could be referred to as aster. This should at least open our minds to the possibility that Bethlehem's Star was not an astronomical object.

Consider the Star's properties.

1The Star Was Seen in the East

The Wise Men asked Herod "Where is he who has been born king of the Jews? For we saw his star when it rose and have come to worship him." Now stars rise in the East. But the Wise Men had come **from** the East to Jerusalem, so it seems likely that the star appeared in the West. That defies the physical laws of star movement, which is actually caused by the Earth's rotation.

2The Star Disappeared and Reappeared

This is a point that I missed for years. Herod had not seen the Star, because he was not looking for it. The Wise Men, on the other hand, had probably been on high alert, looking for this sign of the Messiah, for perhaps as much as four decades. When the Wise Men consulted Herod, he did not say "Oh, THAT star! I was wondering what it was!" If the Star had been continually shining in the sky for the previous two years, then it would have been the subject of conversation in Jerusalem. The strong suggestion of the Wise Men's account is that the Star appeared for one night only. They saw it, because they were looking for it. Others may have seen it, without realizing its significance. But it was enough to set the Wise Men packing for a journey to Israel.

When the Wise Men left Herod, they expressed surprise at the reappearance of the Star. This surprise would not have been evident if the Star had been there, shining in the sky all along. But this is also not normal behavior for am astronomical object.

3The Star Traveled to Guide Them

Stars do not travel in this way. They especially do not move southeast; Bethlehem is southeast of Jerusalem.

4The Star Stood over the House

A star in the sky will not be able to point out the position of a single house on the ground. Once again, this shows that Bethlehem's Star was not an astronomical object. It was not a "huge ball of flaming gas".

5The Star Appeared at an Exact Time

Notice that Herod did not want a vague idea of when the Star appeared, nor even a date. He wanted the exact time, as this would help him pinpoint this child, so that he could have him destroyed.

So, if we collect these pieces of evidence, what do they tell us? And is there anything in the Bible that can give us a clue as to what this Star was?

I believe the answer to the last question is "Yes!"

Consider these two passages about the time when the Israelites were sojourning in the Wilderness.

> And the LORD went before them by day in a pillar
> of cloud to lead them along the way, and by night
> in a pillar of fire to give them light, that they might
> travel by day and by night. (Exodus 13:21)

> On the day that the tabernacle was set up, the
> cloud covered the tabernacle, the tent of the
> testimony. And at evening it was over the
> tabernacle like the appearance of fire until

morning. So it was always: the cloud covered it by day and the appearance of fire by night. (Numbers 9:15-16)

The Numbers passage is particularly interesting. The cloud by day and the fire by night are representative of the presence of the Shekinah Glory of God. The pillar of fire by night would have been described by any anachronistic passing Greek with the word *aster,* as it was a glow in the atmosphere. And, when camp was pitched, that aster, that pillar of fire, the Shekinah

Glory of God, was over the Tabernacle, because that is where the dwelling of God was.

If this was Bethlehem's Star, then the Wise Men, as Gentiles, had the privilege of experiencing both these occurrences. They were led by the pillar of fire, which had presumably appeared to the in Babylon, and led them along the way from Jerusalem to Bethlehem. And then the pillar of fire rested over the house where Joseph, Mary, and Jesus lived, just as it rested over the Tabernacle in the Wilderness, because that house, like the Tabernacle, was where God was dwelling; God the Son, contracted to a span, as Charles Wesley put it.

> Let earth and heaven combine,
> Angels and men agree,
> To praise in songs divine
> The incarnate Deity,
> Our God contracted to a span,
> Incomprehensibly made man.
>
> He laid his glory by,
> He wrapped him in our clay;
> Unmarked by human eye,
> The latent Godhead lay;
> Infant of days he here became,
> And bore the mild Immanuel's name.

Unsearchable the love
That hath the Saviour brought;
The grace is far above
Or man or angels thought;
Suffice for us that God, we know,
Our God, is manifest below.

He deigns in flesh to appear,
Widest extremes to join;
To bring our vileness near,
And make us all divine:
And we the life of God shall know,
For God is manifest below.

Made perfect first in love,
And sanctified by grace,
We shall from earth remove,
And see his glorious face:
Then shall his love be fully showed,
And man shall then be lost in God.

06. Conclusion: How Did the Wise Men Know?

Conclusion: How Did the Wise Men Know?

We need to summarize how the Wise Men knew to do what they did. Their knowledge was one matter. Another matter was their intention to worship – a motivation which we should not overlook, as it is really the most important aspect of the account.

Did the Wise Men find out what they knew by magic? After all, were they not magicians? No, they were not. Just because *magoi* is the root word of magician does not make them responsible for magic, any more than the use of the word aster legitimizes the condemned practice of astrology.

So did the Wise Men use astrology? Not in the way we understand today. Though they would not have had the ideas of modern astronomers, that did not mean they fully accepted pagan astrology. They wanted, after all, to worship this newborn King of the Jews.

If Balaam was a spiritual "ancestor" of the Wise Men, then perhaps their school had roots in paganism, and practices that the Bible condemns. Yet, I suggest that their school was changed and converted under the leadership of Daniel, whose importance is so great that he is one of Ezekiel's three heroes

(Ezekiel 14:14). And, whatever errors they may have developed in the intervening years, it was God's plan to use them to show that the Messiah was the Messiah of the Gentiles, just as the visit of the Shepherds on the night Jesus was born showed that He was the Messiah of the Jews. And it wonderful that Matthew – the most Jewish of the Evangelists – gives us the Gentile Messiah account, while Luke, the Gentile, gives us the Jewish Messiah account! Jesus is truly the Savior of the whole world.

So the Wise Men's methodology was not magic, nor was it astrology. It was exegesis. It seems apparent that they knew certain key passages and prophecies, and they used what they knew of God's word to search diligently; to seek and to find the Savior.

And that is how we also find the Messiah. We find Him through the pages of His living Word, the Bible. We have so much more light than the Wise Men had, yet they used w hat they had to find Him. We should do likewise, using what God has given us – His holy, complete, authoritative, inerrant, infallible, sufficient word – the Bible.

And this is not a cold word. It is a message of hope, of power, of love, and of grievous, dreadful sins forgiven. I believe the

Star was the pillar of fire, the Shekinah Glory of God. If we come to that pillar of fire, we cannot stand in our own strength. That fire lights up every sin in our lives, and shows us that we have broken God's laws, and are worthy of eternal damnation in Hell.

But that Star is a type of Christ. He is the Shekinah Glory of God. He is the Morning Star. If you have realized your sins condemn you, then know this also – He has made a way so that you do not have to be condemned. He has died on the cross, to take the punishment that you deserve for your sins, so that you, if you throw yourself completely on His trust, might be redeemed from your sins, and spend eternity with Him, in a place that you and I do not deserve.

This is a true saying, written by the Apostle Peter, under the inspiration of the Holy Spirit.

> And we have the prophetic word more fully confirmed, to which you will do well to pay attention as to a lamp shining in a dark place, until the day dawns and the morning star rises in your hearts. (2 Peter 1:19)

Let me conclude this little book by pointing you to what to do next. Maybe you know some godly Christian people, who can talk to you about salvation. Maybe there is a good local church where you live. If not, then contact some friend of mine at:

www.needgod.com

As Peter said, you will do well to pay attention. I pray that the Morning Star will rise in your heart.

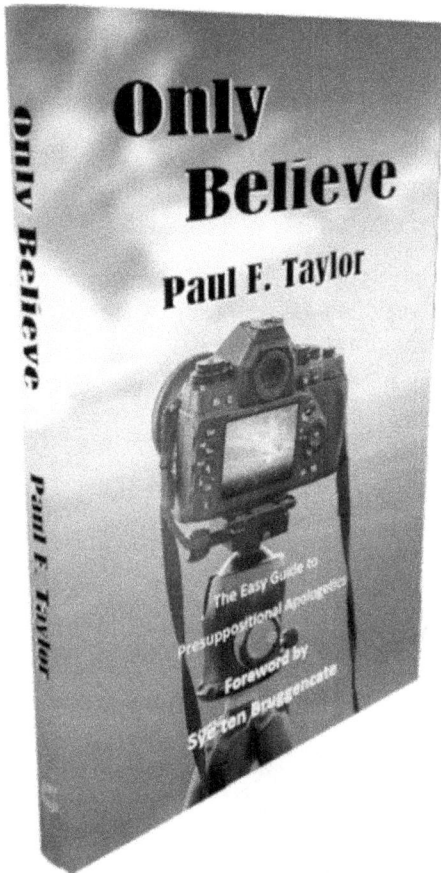

How to build a consistent worldview, based on biblical presuppositions.

Purchase options available at:

https://justsixdays.com/books/only-believe-an-easy-to-follow-guide-to-presuppositional-apologetics/

Mountain Word Science

Mountain Word Science is a new physical science curriculum (i.e. physics and chemistry) for older homeschooled teenagers - approximately grades 10 through 12. Although covering aspects of all levels of the *Trivium*, this course is led by *Rhetorical* principles.

IEach unit begins with Scripture, and frequently refers back to Scripture. The process-led content is heavily influenced by the 1990s English science courses "Salter's Chemistry",and "Salter-Horner Physics", which the author used to teach during the 1990s.

Current Units

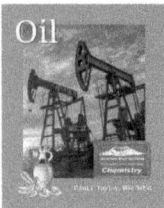

Upcoming Units

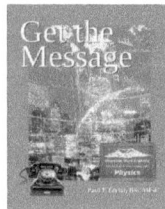

Purchase options at:

https://justsixdays.com/series/mountain-word-science/

How to tell true from false science, by looking at the language used.

Purchase options at:

https://justsixdays.com/books/where-birds-eat-horses-the-language-of-evolution/

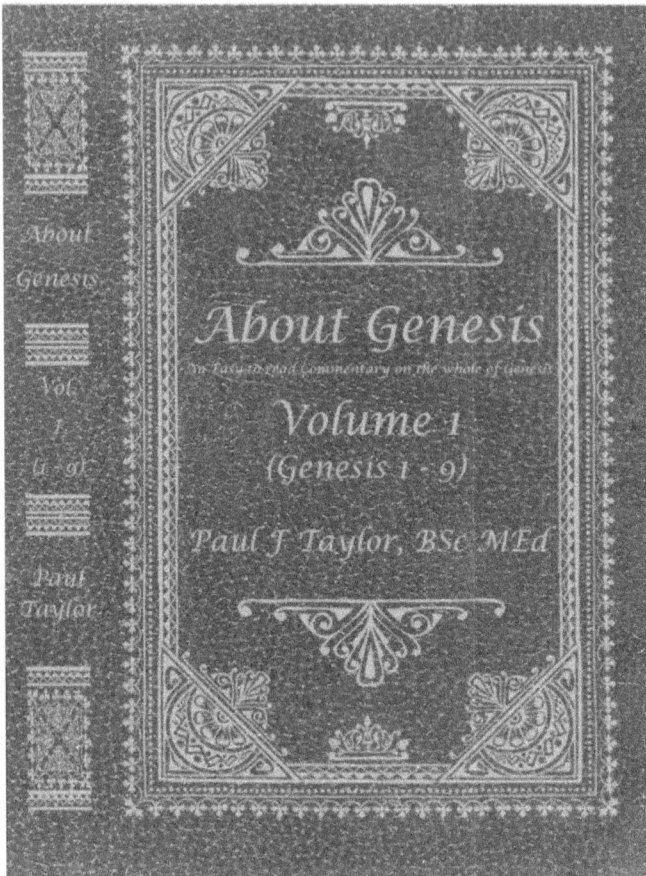

The Creationist commentary on the whole book of Genesis - Volume 1.

Purchase options at:

https://justsixdays.com/books/about-genesis-volume-1/

Help me publish these books:

My next three book projects are:

- About Genesis Vol 2 - half-written

- About Genesis Vol 3 - to finish the series

- A full-length creationist biography of Charles Darwin - title not yet decided

To help buy me time to get these books written, please sponsor me at:

Subscribestar.com/paulftaylor

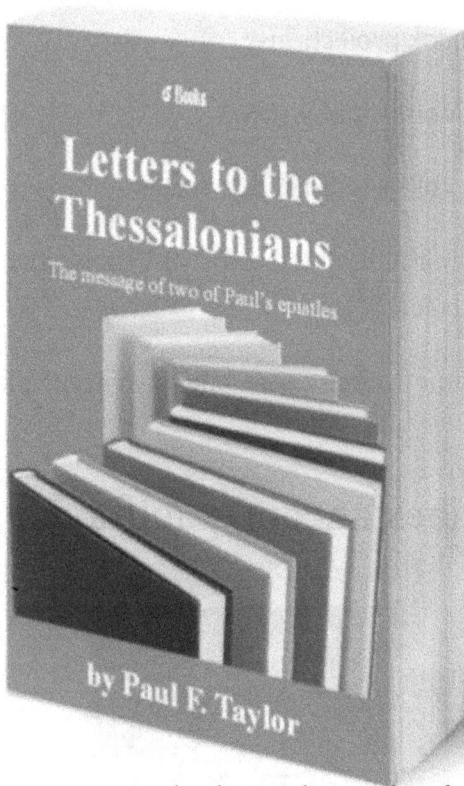

A Commentary on both epistles, with information about the Second Coming of Christ.

Purchase options at:

https://justsixdays.com/books/letters-to-the-thessalonians-the-message-of-two-of-pauls-epistles/

www.ingramcontent.com/pod-product-compliance
Lightning Source LLC
Chambersburg PA
CBHW071929020426
42331CB00010B/2782